Warrior Women: Overcoming the Slayers God's Way

Tammie T. Polk

Laurel, Let God handle it! ♥ Tammie

CONTENTS

Acknowledgments	i
You Are Not Broke!	1
You DO Have Time!	13
Your Family Is Not Stopping You!	23
Your Job Has a Purpose!	33
You're More Than a Side Hustle!	45
No One Is Meant to Be a One Hit Wonder!	57
You're Good? Right...	67
Now What Do I Do?	77
Can You Help Me?	81
Other Books by the Author	84

ACKNOWLEDGMENTS

Father, You've done it again! I will NEVER take my gift of writing for granted! You have blessed me to use the written word in a way that not even I thought was possible!

To my Muse Brigade, my family…your patience with all my writing craziness has been a blessing. Thanks for just shaking your head and laughing! Thanks for letting me continue to inspire the world in my own unique way!

To everyone who has ridden the ride with me: Tameka, Christina, Yalonda, Dana…so many to name! Thank you for giving me the platform to share the vision, for always being there, and for understanding my crazy!

To the naysayers, thank you!

YOU ARE NOT BROKE!

"I'm Broke" is not the final word over your life. Let's get rid of that right now! Being the Broken Business Woman in any area is not your fate. I know that things have been hard and you have seen some lean times. You may even still be in them, but what we're not going to do is allow brokenness to have the final say. You may be temporarily displaced from the comfort that you are used to, but it is not meant to last. I had to learn that.

Girl, you got a story for everything! Yep, I do. And I share them because I want you to understand what is possible and also to show you that I understand where you are coming from.

It was a Sunday afternoon in February and my husband had gone home to get something for a church meeting. I should've known something was wrong when my Dad left, but I didn't think anything of it—until he came back and told my stepmother to take me home while he stayed with our girls. When we got into her truck, she asked me if we had renters' insurance and I immediately started crying. My worst fear had come—our home had been broken into and completely cleaned out from front to back. As much as I tried to look at the bright side of the situation, I couldn't help but worry about my laptop being gone and the tracking software being turned off.

It seemed like I got hit from every direction after that. I lost clients and almost got sued because I had over $11k worth of other people's intellectual property on that laptop. Our peace of mind was shattered and my husband couldn't go to work for days. Our oldest daughter's room was hit the hardest. Everything but her keyboard had been taken. I still remember her sitting in her desk chair and crying because everything she had was gone. Our household routine was thrown off completely and the one computer that wasn't stolen was damaged so bad that it had to be rebuilt. Talk about being broke and broken!

The first thing that I want you to understand is that, even in a situation like that, you're still not broke! There is still a way of escape for you because there are angels on earth! I will not call the names of mine, but I will say this—one of my Facebook friends, who I have yet to meet in real life, organized a gift card campaign on my behalf and we were able to establish a small sense of normalcy in our lives.

So, before you hang your hat on being broke, let me help you to understand where that comes from. First, being broke comes from impatience and uncontrolled impulses. Don't believe me? Let's look to the

Prodigal Son, shall we? (Luke 15:11-32) He knew what he had coming to him, yet he was unwilling to wait for the proper time to receive it. It was his money and he wanted it right then. His father gave it to him and he headed out.

Like anyone with money, he made friends real quick—those fair-weather friends who are nowhere to be found when the money runs out. He lived it up and found himself on the wrong side of the tracks! He had no friends and was homeless. As he walked the streets of the far country he was in, he started missing his water! He took the first job he could as a pig feeder and ate what they ate. After some time, he realized that he needed to make things right with his father.

His older brother tried to talk his father out of helping him, yet his father was more concerned about restoring him now that he'd learned his lesson and returned home. Going home, admitting he was wrong, and restoring the broken relationship was his way out.

Maybe that's not your situation. Okay, let's look at it another way. Being broke can also come from the aftermath of not tithing faithfully. (Malachi 3:8-10, Acts 5) "God knows my heart" is the cliché you'll throw around when you pay your bills with His money. Then you wonder why things go wrong. One thing we must understand about tithing is that the blessings and results of it aren't always monetary. God could have an angel to help you with the physical things that you need to make it. What you already have may last a little bit longer. You may get more time to pay that bill you were worried about. You may not get sick as much or your car seems to no longer be making that noise.

You say you can't afford to tithe and I say that you can't afford not to. It's not about the man that stands in the pulpit where you give it, but about you being obedient to what God has told you to do it. Let Him deal with what happens next. You are to give and then pray that the pastor does right with the money that comes in!

Let's take tithing a step further. What if you really are financially broken and don't have money to give at all, like there is nothing coming in and you are just glad to have a roof over your head. You are still not broke because there is still something that you can do. In the book of Leviticus, when the offerings were first established, God knew that there were some who would not be able to give what He was asking for. What happened? He gave the options so that they could do what He had commanded them to do in making their offerings. (Leviticus 14:21-23) You may not be able to give money, but you have time and the skills and talents that God gave you that could lead to you making the money, allowing you to tithe once again. It's all about how you look at it.

The last thing I want to say here is that you also can't say that you can't do what you need to because you don't have that much. A little boy's lunch in God's hands fed 20k people! (John 6:5-14) Surrounded by doubters and naysayers, he gave the little bit that he had and let God use it. How much more different would our lives be if we did the same thing? It's not about being able to give as much as they next person! God will bless whatever you give.

Think about the widow that put the two mites in the offering. (Luke 21:1-4) Everyone laughed at what she gave and Jesus Himself stood up for her and said that she'd be more blessed than anyone else because she gave everything she had and they gave out of their abundance. God has blessed and will bless those who have what seems like nothing, yet are willing to give anyway.

The widow of Zarephath thought the man of God was crazy when he asked her to make a cake for him before she made one for her and her son. (I Kings 17:8-16) She fought him tooth and nail on that, but eventually did as she was asked. What happened? God moved and she had enough until the day that the drought proclaimed by the man of God ended. How much you want to bet that she was ready for the time when that meal and oil ran out?

See, even in a state of perceived brokenness, you can be preparing and setting yourself up for better days and I'm going to tell you how you can do it. Ready?

- Check yourself! Ask yourself if you are really broke and why.

- Check your spending! What are you really spending your money

5

on? Is it really necessary?

- Check your excuses! Would you be saying that if it were anything else? How is it that you are too broke to serve God?

- If money really is an issue, make a list of 25 things that you know how to do and can make money from. Pick 3 that you can get started on in the next 24 hours and make it happen!

- Ask yourself what you can do until you are able to give financially? What other ways can you serve?

PRAY, PONDER, PLAN, and PROCESS

_____

_____

_____

_____

_____

_____

_____

_____

_____

_____

_____

_____

_____

_____

_____

_____

_____

_____

_____

_____

YOU DO HAVE TIME!

"I don't have time for all that" won't work just like "I'm Broke" won't. Claiming the Time Constrained Business Woman status doesn't excuse it either. Time management is your problem and you need to look at what you are making a priority. Time is the one thing that everyone on earth has the same amount of, yet use very differently.

I know that what I'm about to say is something that many of us are tired of hearing, but if you can go to work or stand in line for hours and days for something material, then you have time to do what God told you to do! Will there be times when you must work on Sunday and may not be able to make it? Yes, there will be; however, getting what God told you to do done even trumps that! Yes, you have to work, but remember that God can still provide for you—just saying!

You can't say that Sunday is the only day that you have to rest and get your errands done when you were living it up from the time you got off on Friday until an hour before church started.

You can't say that you can't be on time for church when you're employee of the month at work. You don't get that by being late nor leaving early.

You can't say that you can't go canvassing with your church to hand out flyers when you are out in the community holding a car wash sign to help your child's sports team raise money.

You can't say that you stand up for too long in church when you're standing in a store line waiting for the store to open so you can get that new phone or new shoes.

It's all about priorities! There is a time and a place for everything and the Bible tells us that in Ecclesiastes 3:1-8, but we don't pay too much attention to that, so let me use the example of Mary and Martha from Luke 16:38-42. Jesus was a guest in their home and Martha was more concerned about being hospitable than with sitting at His feet and being taught. She even went as far as to tell Jesus that He needed to make Mary get up and help her! He checked her and said that Mary had made the right choice. So, how many times have you missed out on what God has for you because you didn't make the time to get where you could sit at His feet and be taught?

Even worse than that, you can think that you have all the time in the world and come back to God when you're ready. You might want to look at the story of the ten virgins in Matthew 25:1-13. Five of the ten spent their time preparing for the bridegroom's arrival and made sure that their lamps were ready with plenty of oil. The other five took their lamps with the oil they had in them and then slept on preparing. Their lack of preparation wasn't the others' problem!

When the bridegroom showed up, their lamps had gone out and they were scrambling for oil. Those that had it refused to share because that meant they wouldn't be ready themselves. So, they went out to buy oil, thinking they could get back in time—NOPE! They ended up being shut out of the marriage supper all because they didn't take the time to prepare.

Thinking that you can delay and spend your time elsewhere will get you caught up every time! Who says that you will have that time? The Bible also tells us that tomorrow is not promised—I know you've heard someone say that at one time or another. Opportunity comes, yet does not always stay.

How many times have you seen an event that you wanted to attend and felt like you had time to get your ticket? You didn't take that moment to purchase your ticket and then you find out that it's sold out. You call the organizer of the event begging for a ticket and they tell you that there's nothing that they can do. Now, you're mad at them because they won't do something about how you chose to spend your time and what you made a higher priority. People have deadlines for a reason.

How can you do better with decisions that affect the time that you have to do things? Here are three things I need you to look at:

- Are you managing your time or wasting it? There is a difference. When you are managing your time, you are purposely and intentionally getting things done that are truly important. When you are wasting your time, you will spend time doing things that have no value and then be upset when the aftermath of not getting key things done comes down on you.

- Ask yourself what it's really time for? There are things that you really are supposed to be doing. Are you doing them? Before you start your day, ask yourself this question.

- How do you view downtime? Do you think that you don't have any?

PRAY, PONDER, PLAN, and PROCESS

_____

_____

_____

_____

_____

_____

_____

_____

_____

_____

_____

_____

_____

_____

_____

_____

_____

_____

YOUR FAMILY IS NOT STOPPING YOU!

"I have a family, so I have to put what God told me to do on hold." No, ma'am, you can't claim that nor take on the traits of the Family Distracted Business Woman. When God has something that He wants you to do, your family is a part of that and is the reason that you are doing it. How so? You are setting an example for them as to what it means to serve God! When you show them that it's not important, they will grow up thinking that it's not. (Ephesians 6)

I'm going to skip the personal life examples here and go straight to the Bible on this one. And I'm going to start with the queen of marriage and family, the Virtuous Woman of Proverbs. There are 21 reasons listed as to why what you're trying to force down people's throats doesn't hold water! This woman had a family and she:

- Knew her value—she knew who she was and how special she was (vs. 10)

- Took care of her husband's physical needs (vs.11)

- Treated her husband with the utmost respect (vs. 12)

- Worked with her hands and stayed busy (vs. 13)

- Helped provide for her home and made sure her family was fed (vs.14)

- Managed and supervised others and met their needs as well (vs. 15)

- Owned property and lived off the land (vs. 16)

- Took care of herself (vs. 17)

- Put out her best work and worked long hours (vs. 18)

- Knew how to sew and make things (vs. 19)

- Gave to the poor and helped the community (vs. 20)

- Prepared her family for the changing of the seasons (vs. 21)

- Was well dressed (vs. 22)

- Spoke highly of her husband (vs. 23)

- Made money from the things she made (vs. 24)

- Was a woman of inner strength and honor (vs. 25)

- Knew what she was talking about and how to talk to people (vs. 26)

- Kept her house clean (vs. 27)

- Was an example to her children and a crown to her husband (vs. 28)

- Lived with a spirit of excellence (vs. 29)

- Feared God (vs. 30)

- Didn't have to sound off about what she was doing (vs. 31)

One thing that we forget is that we serve God through serving our families. Every command given to the woman in the Bible can be summed up right here! None of these 21 things is going to keep you from serving God. Don't believe that?

The money that you make from selling the things that you make would be the income that you tithe from—a way to serve God. You have the opportunity to share your faith with those that you work with and when you are out there working in the community—another way to serve God. Being a good steward as far as your home is concerned—that's serving God. Learning to fear God is going to lead to a desire to serve Him.

You having a family is not going to trump the call and assignment that God has on your life! If it did, the Bible would not exist because, Honey, people in the Bible had some serious family problems! Let's look at some:

- Cain killed his brother.

- Canaan spied on his father Noah while he was naked.

- Absalom slept with this father David's concubines.

- Amnon raped his own sister.

- Abraham had a child with another woman at the request of his wife.

- Rachel and Leah had a whole competition going for Jacob's

affection by having a baby race.

- Joseph's brothers got so jealous that they sold him into slavery and then lied to their father about what happened to him.

Despite ALL OF THAT, God used the people in these situations to do remarkable things, so don't think that your family dynamic is going to render you unable to serve God, because it won't. God established the family so that His work COULD be done! And, there are some people in the Bible that made things happen without having a family because God told them not to have a family – look at the life of Jeremiah.

Notice also that the family was established before anything else—the church, government, etc. So, if it was a burden, then why would he place such a high premium on it from the beginning? Even the animal families were established before the human family! God looked at Adam and said he needed what the animals had, so He made Eve and then they had children. Everything else came AFTER the family!

I'll leave you with this one question: Are you taking the time to equip your family so that they can help you in your service to God?

PRAY, PONDER, PLAN, and PROCESS

YOUR JOB HAS A PURPOSE!

Would you believe me if I told you that I didn't have notes for this one? Oh well! I can still give you the business, though! "I have a job" won't keep you from doing what God told you to do, if you don't let it—I'll talk about that in a minute. Being the Job Insecure Business Woman isn't your lot in life either! Even though, in this day and time, job security seems to be a thing of the past, your job still has a purpose! Everything that you're learning and being exposed to is something that you will use later on in life.

I didn't realize how true this was until I was in college. Putting things in alphabetical order was one of those things that I never thought I would use in life ever again. Man, was I WRONG! I was working in the financial aid office and my job was to prep the academic suspension and probation letters to go out and to refile the files the counselors used when meeting with students. There were at least ten file cabinets in that room, grouped by student classification. Everyone laughed at me because I would be humming the ABC song as I put files back in their proper place.

The Bible can check us here, too, with the attitude that we have towards our jobs. Let's start with this "come late, leave early" mentality that runs through our blood. That's a part of being a good steward of our jobs. I Corinthians 4:2 tells us that we are to be FOUND faithful. What does that mean? It means that we are coming to work on time! When the day starts, you should be in your place ready to work, no matter how much you don't want to be there. "Beginning with the end in mind" should not be the mantra that carries you throughout the day!

When I go into a store and see a cashier with that look on their faces, I ask them how much long they have on their shift. Their whole mood changes as they either tell me what time they get off or how many hours, minutes, and seconds they have left. I even saw one girl with a countdown timer going on her phone for the end of her shift! Now, I'm not saying that I don't understand that the people, places, and things going on in your job won't take you there. I know that you are praying your strength in the LORD to make it through without checking that coworker who continues to come for you or that boss who seems to think you're an octopus; however, you have to remember that YOU need to be FOUND faithful.

When you are focused on being found faithful, time will go by a lot faster! Try it and see. Once you find out what is on your plate for the day, pray and get after it. Develop the tunnel vision that it takes to get what is tasked for you done. Ask God to order your steps and to close your mouth! No, I'm not saying that you should be a doormat, but I am saying that you should pray that He would guide the words that come from the pinkie toe when that coworker or boss comes at you!

The next thing I want to talk about is that half-hearted effort you give to your job every day. You know I'm telling the truth and that you are the POSTER CHILD for doing just enough to get by. You do just enough for "nobody to say anything to me." Is that really how you want your life to be set up? Ecclesiastes 9:10 tells us this: "Whatsoever they hand findeth to do, do it with thy might; for there is no work, nor device, nor knowledge, not wisdom in the grave, whither thou goest." That alone should let you know that doing enough to get by is not going to cut it! It is a temporary solution that was cause a permanent problem.

When you put your all into what you are to do on a given day, you have to do so despite not being acknowledged for it. You will have those days when not one person mentions how hard you worked or the effort that you put into getting things done. Learn to celebrate and reward yourself, keeping in mind that there may be people watching and that things are revealed in unexpected ways. I'll give you an example.

A principal in a school I contract for is known for walking the building, watching what's going on in the classrooms. When she sees a teacher fully engaged and doing something awesome, she takes note of it. As soon as that teacher is out of their classroom, she goes back and leaves them a note of encouragement and praise, along with a little treat to help them get through the day. She did it for me one day.

I had taken on a classroom for an entire semester and worked my tail off to keep those kids going until their new teacher came the next semester. As I closed out for Christmas break, I was presented with an envelope and told not to open it until I was home. In that envelope was that note of encouragement and praise along with several restaurant gift cards—one for my husband and I and one for the kids! Even though I took an extended amount of time off between assignments, that made me want to work that much harder when I came back.

The problem is that some don't think that way. They are more like the unjust steward in Luke 16! They are wasting their time goofing off and playing on the clock. They do the little bit they are going to do for a couple of hours and then blow off the rest of the time. When word gets to the boss, they scramble to try to look like they're doing something and it's obvious that they haven't been doing anything. Now, they are fighting to keep their job and it didn't even have to go down like that. All the people they snap at are now the people that they are asking to help them get stuff done. They offer a half-hearted apology and beg for them to help get them out of the jam they put themselves in. "I was just playin' when I said that..." yeah...let me move on.

As I tell people often, You have to remember that your job can be your first step and how you act determines how far you go! Let me put it to you this way: if the person with the key to your next step was standing in front of you, would they give it to you? While you are complaining about getting passed over for a higher position, it just might be because that person has been watching you and felt as though they couldn't give you the job! There is no one to blame for that but YOU! Your attitude, drive, and work ethic can keep you from getting a lot of what you are looking for from your job…

Here are a few things you need to think about:

- Ask this question: If this were my company, how would I make it better? The answer to that question could be used to build what God has put in you to do!

- Realize that you're letting down your biggest investor by not giving your all at work! If you are working in order to save so you can do what God wants you to do, losing your job for being shaky and flaky is going to stop all of that!

- Understand that the opportunities you are privy to in your job have been shared with you for a reason. Would you believe me if I told you that there will be times when people will see that you aren't meant to be there and will start sending things your way that will help you get out there and do what you need to do?

I'll end this chapter with a memory. A woman started taking side jobs, which she was being given by her boss. She didn't understand why he was doing something that was clearly against company policy, yet she continued to serve in excellence. Three months later, she was told that a merger with another company meant that she would lose her job! She now knew why her boss did what he did. She was able to sustain herself with those side jobs and in turn built her own business.

Sweetheart, YOUR JOB HAS A PURPOSE!

PRAY, PONDER, PLAN, and PROCESS

_____

_____

_____

_____

_____

_____

_____

_____

_____

_____

_____

_____

_____

_____

_____

_____

_____

_____

_____

_____

_____

_____

Tammie T. Polk

YOU'RE MORE THAN A SIDE HUSTLE!

We live in a world where the Talent Starved Business Woman is being intentionally created by the greed of those whom we work for daily. While this may be happening, it is not the mode that you are meant to be in right now. I know how it is…

Your job starts to get on your nerves. You start looking for something else, but everything you see is worse than what you have. Someone tells you that you should be doing this or that. You believe them and start making things happen. You start to make money, yet you aren't putting your heart into it because you still feel like you owe your job every ounce of creativity that's in you. You start to fall off. People ask you why you stopped. You say that it was just something you did for a hot second, knowing full well that it would be so much more if you gave it the time and energy it deserved. Yet, you are content to be a professional clean up girl!

I compare you to the man with the one talent in Matthew 25:24-30. Why? It's because you did just what he did—you took your one talent and buried it in the sand because you were afraid of what would come of it. You came up with every excuse you possibly could for why you didn't make more out of it, all while watching those who once supported you now spending their money elsewhere! Now, you find yourself scrambling to get things going again so that you can get back into their good graces…but it may be too late. You may be headed right for that utter darkness of being shelved because you didn't use what God gave you while the window was open.

Or, maybe you are the one who thinks that you're doing all you can and will suffer if you go any further, let alone help someone else! The widow in I Kings 17 looked at Elijah like he had three heads when he told her to make him a cake first and then feed herself and her son. All she did was tell him how she couldn't do it, how it was her last, and how they would die after they were done because it was all they had. Sound familiar? When it comes to using our talents to help others, we can be the same way. You may be barely making it and then someone asks you to donate something, participate in an event, or something like that—you look at what YOU can't do without looking up and asking for help from on high to get it done!

Yes, the person asking knows that you don't have much…

Yes, the person asking knows that you would get in trouble if your job found out, yet they keep telling you the impact you would have…

Yes, the person asking knows that you're in dire straits, but they wouldn't have come to you if they didn't think you could do it!

There will be days when you will see someone who you can help with the talent that you have and it will truly cost you. However, if it even looks like it's within your power, with God's help, to get it done, you should! Let's go back to this widow.

She did what Elijah told her to do and probably complained the entire time, yet because of her obedience, God stepped in and she not only made it through that day, but for many days to come! What will God do when you decide to be obedient? Keep in mind the old hymn, "Little is much when God is in it. Labor not for wealth or fame. There's a crown and you can win it, if you'll go in Jesus' name!"

Still not you? Then maybe you are like Simon, the fisherman in Luke 5: 4-11. You've been working all night with no results! Nothing that you do is working and then someone comes along, telling you to do something you've already done. Like Simon, you tell them that you tried that and they encourage you to try again. They won't let up, though...so you force yourself to do it and God MOVES! You will need help, just as Simon did, to handle all that is coming your way and then pray, asking God for forgiveness because you doubted what He could do! He smiles and tells you that He's not done with you yet and gives you another assignment...you say yes, follow Him, and turn the world upside down and right side up at the same time!

Tammie, you haven't gotten to me yet! I'm enjoying what I'm reading, but you're still outside my wheelhouse. I have two more people I want you to meet...

First, would be Gideon. You see, Gideon was the red headed step child in his family...that one who people said wouldn't amount to anything. In Judges 6, God reveals Himself to Gideon and tells him what He needs him to do. What does Gideon do? He basically tells God He's got the wrong dude and begins to question and test God, all while begging for his life in the process. When he finally wraps his head around what God is telling him, he slowly lets go of the reins.

See, we can be a lot like Gideon. God will reveal something to us and we say, "Wayment, God! Do you know who you're asking to do that? You DO know who I am, right?" God shakes His head, chuckles, and says, "Yes, ma'am! I'm talking to YOU!" We look at God sideways and wonder if He's really serious...and He is indeed! Then, once He starts telling you what His vision for you is, you say, "You're going to have to show me how I'm supposed to get this done because I don't see it." He says okay and commences to do so, blowing your mind!

You start to notice how much things start to change. He starts removing people, places and things from your life so that you can do what He told you to do—all you can do is sit by in silence and be obedient. When you follow His leading, you take down giants! The little vision you had for what your talents could produce has become mighty! It is for this reason that I say you are more than a side hustle, my friend! Oh, and did I mention that

Gideon is mentioned in the Hall of Faith in Hebrews 11?

Earlier, I mentioned a widow looking at what she had and not seeing the big picture, but the Disciples had the same problem when Jesus said the crowd He had just preached to needed to eat. We all know the story of the two fishes and five loaves of bread, yet we don't pay attention to what Jesus did. In Luke 9:11-17, He shows us how to handle what we have. He took it, prayed over it, and trusted God to do something powerful! Over twenty thousand people ate from that! Think about it: there were five thousand MEN. Let's just say that every man there was married and had a family. I truly believe that there were more than five thousand there.

When Jesus told them to gather up what was left, there were twelve baskets of food and the people had eaten until they could eat no more! Imagine having that spillover in your life and then using that excess to go forward and help someone else.

Look at the fact that you didn't have to spend another dime to prepare for the next show of talent.

Look at the fact that you have exactly what you need to get the job done.

Look at the fact that God prepared you for the next yes—and all you had to do was be obedient!

I need to end this chapter before I start shouting and not finish this book! Here are some things I want you to focus on and implement:

- Grow your talents! Never miss an opportunity to learn, no matter how much you think you already know. There is always something new coming out that's related to your talent and there is always room to improve and grow!

- Use your talents in God's service! I am woman enough to admit that I have failed here and still struggle with it some. Don't let what others say about what God has put in you to do keep you from using your talents to serve Him. What God put in you is meant to save someone's life, ministry, business, or family...and you need to understand that. If you feel opposition, pray, pay attention, and move forward. Realize and understand that He gave it to you to give back to Him!

- Is what you're doing really a talent? You can be good at something and it not be a talent. A talent is something that you know how to do and enjoy doing, not something that you know how to do and dread doing. There is an ENORMOUS difference!

- Ask yourself if you are managing or wasting your talents. Be real with yourself...I hate to do this to you, but if you want to know the difference, you'll have to read the other Slayers book!

PRAY, PONDER, PLAN, and PROCESS

_____

_____

_____

_____

_____

_____

_____

_____

_____

_____

_____

_____

_____

_____

_____

_____

_____

_____

_____

_____

Tammie T. Polk

NO ONE IS A ONE-HIT WONDER!

No matter what the term means, you are NOT the One-Hit Wonder Business Woman, either! Even Jesus was known for more than preaching…come on, now! You know better than that…and you know you do.

Maybe you're feeling that way because you're having a Moses moment. You're so focused on what you can't do that you don't see that you were spared a lot of things for a reason. You were hidden away because of the promise that God had on your life. You've been molded and shaped to truly deliver people, yet you look at what you don't have, can't do, etc. Moses was meant to be more than just a son of Pharaoh. Although he enjoyed all the benefits of doing so, there was more needed out of his life…as it is with yours!

In Exodus 3, God tells Moses what it is he is meant to do, yet all he has known was being one of the richest rulers in Egypt who fled after killing an Egyptian. God told him what his more was and Moses couldn't handle it! Is that you? Do you know what your more is, yet you can't wrap your head around what God wants you to do? If it was meant for you to figure out, then you wouldn't need God to get it done! That's why He specializes in the impossible.

Notice that nothing God told Moses to do was anything he already knew how to do. Moses said he couldn't speak and God reminded him that He made him then gave him Aaron to help him. Moses said he wouldn't know what to say and God gave him the words and the script to read from, too. Moses said that he didn't know how to lead and God told him that He would be with him!

Once Moses took his place, things became difficult because people only knew him as that rich ruler who killed that Egyptian. They mocked him and said that he was no leader. Now, that would stop most people and I am sure Moses struggled, yet Moses went on and became the deliverer of Egypt with God's help.

Don't let your Moses moment cheat you out of the more in your life. Yes, you may be doing all fine and good with that one thing that you know how to do, yet God is going to call you into account for EVERY ability He gave you and not just that one. Do you really want to stand before Him one day and say that you let your more go to the dogs because of what you wouldn't trust Him to help you do?

Or, maybe you're like Rahab and feel that you will never be more than you are. She was known as the town prostitute, yet she had the foresight to hid the Israeli spies when they came to down. People may look at you and wonder why God would use someone like you, but it's not their business, nor it is yours! You are to do what God told you to do…PERIOD!

A pastor was asked how he built his church and he said from helping others to overcome and then sending them back out to where they came from to help others. People cringed when the said he had a prostitute ministry, a stripper ministry, etc. and he had very little support because of that. What people didn't see was that he was stepping into his more. Once people were healed, he encouraged them to go out and bring in whoever they could. When they came, he offered them the same help and counsel that he gave those who brought them in. This pastor was not JUST a pastor—he had turned entire communities around for the Lord and he didn't care what anyone thought!

Even though everyone knew who Rahab was and what she did, she knew that hiding them was the right thing to do. She knew what God was about do where she lived. In Joshua 2, she confessed to the spies that she believed what she heard about God and wanted her household to be spared. In order to do so, she had to do more! They told her what to do and she had to be ready! Ready for what? To be the great-grandmother of King David and in the lineage of Jesus Himself! When she stepped into her more, big things happened…so, who are you to think that you are meant to be a one-hit wonder? If Moses and Rahab can turn things around with

God's help, so can you!

Paul would be an extreme case. When God started to use him, everybody thought he was suspect! People were afraid to go near him because all they could think about was being arrested or killed for serving God. This was a mocker and persecutor of the church. He killed Christians for sport. Surely, God couldn't turn around and use someone like Him! We wouldn't have over half the Bible if Paul didn't step into his more, which he did in Acts 9. He didn't buck up against God! He said, "Lord, what wilt thou have me to do?" When God told him, he did it!

Your more, better and greater is waiting right on the other side of your obedience. The only thing I want you to think is this: Be like Paul! Once God reveals what your more is, don't buck against Him! Go into town, see the people He tells you to see, and go forward in His name. You know what He has for you to do. You know there is so much more you could be doing.

Don't worry about those who say you shouldn't…

Nor those who say you can't…

Nor those who say you won't…

Nor those who laugh…

It's not worth your more!

PRAY, PONDER, PLAN, and PROCESS

Tammie T. Polk

_____

_____

_____

_____

_____

_____

_____

_____

_____

_____

_____

_____

_____

_____

_____

_____

_____

_____

_____

_____

_____

_____

_____

_____

_____

Tammie T. Polk

YOU'RE GOOD? RIGHT...

Unbelievably, the Sad and Settled Business Woman isn't always sad. Nope! She can be just like the rich ruler in Luke 12:16-21. She can have everything she needs and then some. She can have more money than she knows what to do with and upgrading everything she has in every way possible. She's got life insurance, savings, multiple 401k and retirement accounts, businesses of her own, children on full rides to college, debt paid off, and LIVING—but she is GODLESS! She thinks having all of that IS God when it's not!

You can have everything in the world and it is MEANINGLESS without God, sweetheart! When you forget Him, you have NOTHING! As God said to this man in verse twenty, "But God said unto him, Thou fool, this night they soul shall be required of thee: then whose shall those things be, which thou hast provided?" In other words, he had gained the world and lost his soul!

Honey, no matter what way you look at this thing, you're not "good" at all and you know that something is missing. You think that God is blessing you because things are going well for you and you are lying to yourself and everyone else you tell that lie to along the way! In His eyes, you are still a baby in need of milk, though you think you're eating meat...why are you settling for "good?"

Now, let me say this—none of what you have going for you is a bad thing! I'm not going to say that it is and let me apologize now if you felt that way. I'm not downplaying your hustle and drive, I'm challenging you to look at the source. If you have all of this and are telling yourself that you are good without God, you are in for a hard road!

Let me tell you what happened to me. Life and business were GOOD! We had moved into a new home and I was making a profit from my business. I had one client whose monthly payment paid all of my business bills, which meant everything else that came in went to the house. I was so wrapped up in the good that was happening that I wasn't honoring God at all! I wasn't tithing, scheduled sessions that kept me out of church, and more, yet I thought I was good and that He was blessing me...

That was when I got the text message that nearly stopped my heart. The client that paid all of my business bills cancelled her contract with me. She said she could no longer afford to work with me. This started a domino effect and I ended up losing every client I had. When I reached out to my mentor to talk about it, tithing was the first thing she asked me about and I shook my head. I reached out to another friend and she asked me the same question...

Your all is nothing if you're not honoring God with it. I know that sounds harsh, yet it is true. So, are you really "good" or are you starting to take a long, hard, honest look at your life?

Or, maybe you're on the other side. Because of the hand life dealt you, you don't want to be known or seen at all and live your life thinking about yesterday. You feel that God has forgotten you, Naomi, but He hasn't! Naomi lost her husband and her sons in one fell swoop. Then, there was a famine in the land. She looked at her daughters in law and sent them away. She had nothing else for them. When she got to where she was going, bitterness set in and she told people to call her Mara, which means bitter! She went on and on about how God had dealt with her and she was miserable! The book of Ruth tells her story. Take a moment and look at what God did....

One key thing I want to point out is that God is working even when it seems like everything around you is going wrong. Boaz didn't just fall out of the sky, Ruth and Naomi were led to him—this was God's doing! Sometimes the way our lives are set up is just what God needs to work as only He can! When Ruth told Naomi who she met, she couldn't believe it...and their lives changed immediately! You never know who you're being led to that is meant to be a blessing to you. You may be in a pit, but you don't have to settle in and decorate it!

It is good to remember yesterday, but not at the expense of today's vision. Going back to Egypt isn't an option for you because God brought you out for a reason. You can't do what He needs you to do when you're in Egypt, so why are you trying to go back there? The purpose of yesterday is for you to understand what God has done for you and to encourage you to continue to move forward. Yesterday is a reminder of who you no longer are because He brought you out!

It is time for you to grow! Here is what I want you to do:

- Ask yourself this question: What will happen if I don't get things right? You may have to give up some things in order to do so, but your relationship with God is worth everything that it takes. Plus, He will restore it!

- Ask yourself another question: "Am I really good?" I want you to think about it because you can be so earthly consumed that you are heavenly bankrupt!

- Ask yourself this final question: What is God telling me to do? God does not do stuck, stale, nor stagnant, which is why He compels us to GROW!

PRAY, PONDER, PLAN, and PROCESS

_____

_____

_____

_____

_____

_____

_____

_____

_____

_____

_____

_____

_____

_____

_____

_____

_____

_____

_____

_____

NOW WHAT DO I DO?

If you're feeling like you've had a second encounter with the Slayers, then that's a good thing! In this chapter, I'm going to share with you seven more Slayers that are bound to come up if you aren't careful in your journey as a Warrior Woman. I was going to put out another book, but I am going to include them here. Think of them as fiery arrows that you need to put up your shield and protect yourself from.

- I'm not ready or not there yet—If you wait until you're ready, then you're going to watch greatness pass you by! What is it that is stopping you from starting today? Is it really stopping you or do you not just want to do it? You don't have to have the best and the brightest right now, but, as my friend Christina says, THE WORLD NEEDS YOUR START!

- I have to take care of my family first—Your family is the reason you're doing it in the first place, so remember that! You can't provide for them if you don't take care of YOU! Always remember that you yourself are your first and primary business. YOU MATTER! If you continue to feed the dreams of others, there will be nothing left for you to do anything for yourself. I know that you want to help your family do get things done, but you have to make sure that you can do what's in your heart and mind to do as well!

- That's not for me—Okay, first let me say that there is a time where you will be right about this because you know who you are, what you can do, and what you want to be involved in. That part, I get. What I don't get is when you say that in reference to something that you KNOW will help you to do more, better, and greater and you turn in Jonah and run away from it. You'll say that God closed the door or that God has you on another assignment and you don't have time to do that—and you'll be LYING THROUGH YOUR TEETH! You don't want to do it because it requires you to be comfortable with being uncomfortable. You don't want to get out of bed, spend the money on that instead of on your hair and nails, watch videos or read books about it, etc. You want the easy road and what God has put in your heart to do ain't easy and never will be. It's not that it's not for you…you're just LAZY!

- I've got time—No, ma'am, you don't! You never know when God is going to call your name. Les Brown said it best when he said that the graveyard is the richest place on earth! I bet you can think of someone who has passed on before they saw what they said they wanted to do come to fruition. Do you want that to be you? As I have said before, opportunities expire, prices go up, things go out of stock or on backorder—anything can happen. Is that a chance you really want to take? It's time to pray, ponder, and prioritize because you DON'T have all the time in the world.

- It doesn't take all that—Keep telling yourself that! I'm reminded of the man who told his son to build a house. He decided that he would impress his future father-in-law by taking short cuts and saving money. He did what he was asked to do with as little as possible. When he finished the house, the man said, "Congratulations, son! You just built your wedding present." The young man's heart sank because he was so caught up in taking those short cuts that he built something that was subpar—and now he had to live in it!

- I'm not qualified—According to who? Moses didn't think he was qualified to do what God asked him to do, either. Stop looking at the fact that you don't have a piece of paper saying what you can do. I'll be the first to tell you that doesn't matter. Don't believe me? Take an example from my life: I get paid to come in and turn around classrooms where degreed, certified professionals are unable to keep up. I get called to clean up the mess many times—and I am not licensed, certified, highly qualified or any of that. I am a woman with a particularly desirable skill set who found a way to use it! Honey, so are you, so stop keeping yourself from being GREAT!

- I have no support—I didn't either in the beginning. My question to you is this: Is it more important for you to have support or is it more important for you to use what God put in you to save someone's life, family, ministry, and/or business? You may not have those closest to you rooting for you. You might be Jesus like me. What does the Bible say? He came unto His own and His own received Him not! If it didn't stop Jesus, don't let it stop you! Also know that your support can and will come from other places. Many of my biggest supporters are women on Facebook who I have yet to meet in real life! They are my Angels and I thank God for them!

I want to challenge you to change your mindset before you sink any further because, if you don't, the message of this book will leave you as soon as you close it…It's time to get prepared for what you know God has put in you to share with the world!

CAN YOU HELP ME?

Yes, I can! I am here to lovingly annoy you into greatness and I mean that with everything in me! Here are a few of the things that I offer:

- Every Woman Is a Business Woman Boot Camp and Kickstart Accountability Program
  - o 8 week coaching program
    - ▪ 30 Day Boot Camp answering the questions of who, what, when, where, why, how, and how much in respect to what you have in your heart and mind to do
    - ▪ 4 Week Kickstart Accountability Program where we take one major project and make it happen in 4 weeks!
  - o You will receive both the electronic and print copies of my book, Every Woman Is a Business Woman: A 30 Day Boot Camp for the Real Business Woman
- From Your Heart to Paper Author's Intensive
  - o VIP Day Experience

- Learn how I self published more than 20 books in three years, all while being a married, homeschooling mother of three girls who runs two businesses, works as a substitute teacher, and has a husband who works the night shift.

- Learn how I took one funny childhood memory and turned it into an e-book, a 30-day Facebook live series, a 30-day online group coaching program, print book, workshop, and retreat experience.

  o I will also help you with the book set up and publishing process—editing, proofreading, and getting the right size book template

- Virtuous and Real Business Woman Book Coaching Program

  o 12-week coaching program

    - Choose the book you want to use, even this one!

    - 12 one-hour video or phone calls working through the book you choose from cover to cover

  o You will receive an autographed copy of the book along with a few surprises

- Transitioning to Home and Homeschool Program
  - o Get help setting up routines and processes to help you to be able to run your business and homeschool your children at the same time!

You can access all of these programs from my website's Work with Me page or you can shoot me an email or Facebook message—that works, too! I do travel with these things, so if you are looking for something in person for your group, job, business, or church, I will come out and facilitate these for you!

OTHER BOOKS BY THE AUTHOR

Here is what I have published as of 5/24/18:

- Personal Perspective Project: Are You the Jealous One/ #ShadeDisguised: I Really Don't Like Y'all

- From One King's Daughter to Another devotional books:
    - Understanding Your Value (tween and teen girls)
    - Becoming a Woman of Virtue (adult women)

- Virtuous and Distinguished Collection
    - The Virtuous Business Woman: Inspired by Proverbs 31
    - The Distinguished Business Man: What a Man in Business Can Learn from Proverbs 31
    - The 7 Virtuous Business Woman Slayers: 7 Deadly Copouts

- Prayerfully Paying Attention: 8 Areas Where We Lose Ourselves

- Slaying the Slayers to Become a Virtuous Business Woman: Overcoming the 7 to Gain the 21

- Putting Your Choices in Check (homeschool)

- Getting Rid of That Babypreneur Mentality: It's Time to GROW UP!

- Every Woman Is a Business Woman: A 30 Day Boot Camp for the Real Business Woman

- The Real Business Women Slay Slayers SuperBook Series

  o The Broken Business Woman

  o The Time Constrained Business Woman

  o The Family Distracted Business Woman

  o The Job Insecure Business Woman

  o The Talent Starved Business Woman

  o The One Hit Wonder Business Woman

  o The Sad and Settled Business Woman

- Rise. Reclaim. Evolve: Breaking It Down for the Woman Wanting Change

- Fiction Books

  o The Last Escapade

  o Becoming Mai

ABOUT THE AUTHOR

Wife and mother.
Homeschool parent and consultant.
Substitute teacher.
Author.
Speaker.
Virtual assistant.
Business woman.

Tammie T. Polk resides in Memphis, TN, and began writing at the age of eleven. After her sixth grade teacher admonished her mother to never stop her from writing, she began writing stories to entertain her friends. She wrote two books during her teenage years, yet her first published book would not come until September 2015. From there, Tammie has gone on to write 23 books on life, family, faith, and business—all while providing workshops, 1:1 and group coaching sessions, and hosting local expos, traveling the country speaking at women's empowerment events, being a part of Toastmasters International and WomanSpeak, and hosting an international radio show.

When she's not taking over the world, you can find Tammie playing games, wrestling with her kids, and watching cartoons! She says that writing is her cross and she takes it seriously!